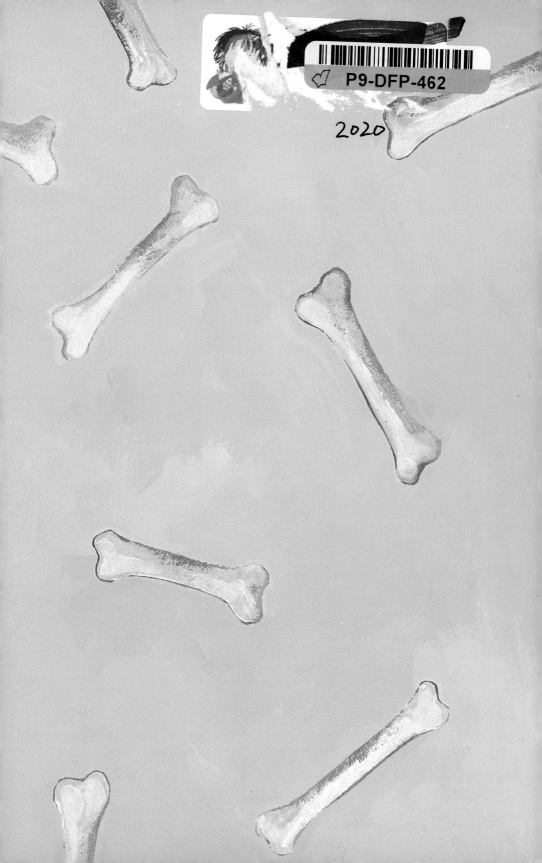

2020

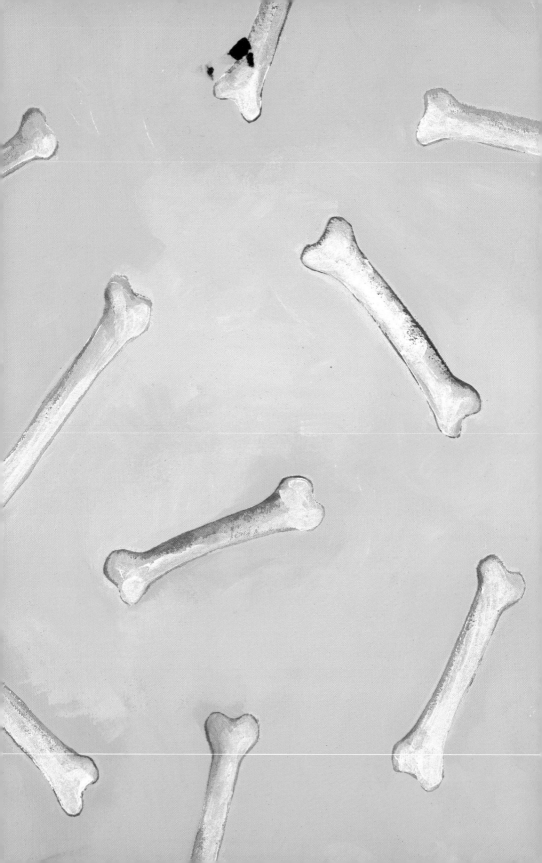

HONEY HELPS

HAPPY HONEY

HONEY HELPS

written by **Laura Godwin**
pictures by **Jane Chapman**

MARGARET K. McELDERRY BOOKS
NEW YORK · LONDON · TORONTO · SYDNEY · SINGAPORE

Margaret K. McElderry Books
An imprint of Simon & Schuster Children's Publishing Division
1230 Avenue of the Americas, New York, NY 10020

The text of this book was set in Century Schoolbook.
The illustrations were rendered in acrylic.
Printed and bound in the United States of America.

2   4   6   8   10   9   7   5   3

Library of Congress Cataloging-in-Publication Data
Godwin, Laura.
Honey helps / by Laura Godwin ; illustrated by Jane Chapman.   p. cm.
Summary: Honey the cat is determined to help Happy the dog
bury his bone, even though he does not want any help.
ISBN 0-689-83407-1
[1. Dogs—Fiction. 2. Cats—Fiction.]
I. Chapman, Jane, ill. II. Title. III. Series.
PZ7.G5438   Ho 2000   [e]—dc21   99-46924

Here is Happy.
Happy has a bone.

Here is Honey.

Honey wants
a bone, too.

Go away, Honey.

This bone
is not for you.

See Happy.

Happy can dig.

Happy can dig
a big hole.

See Honey.

Honey can dig.

Honey can dig
a little hole.

No, no, Honey!
You cannot dig here.

Go away, Honey!

Honey will not go away.

Honey wants
to help Happy.

No, no, Honey!

Happy does not want help.

Go away, Honey!

Happy digs and digs.

Happy digs a big hole.

Happy puts the bone in.

Honey digs and digs.

Honey digs a little hole.

Honey takes the bone out.

Look, Happy!

Honey has a bone.

Honey has a bone
for you!

Happy Happy.

Happy Honey!

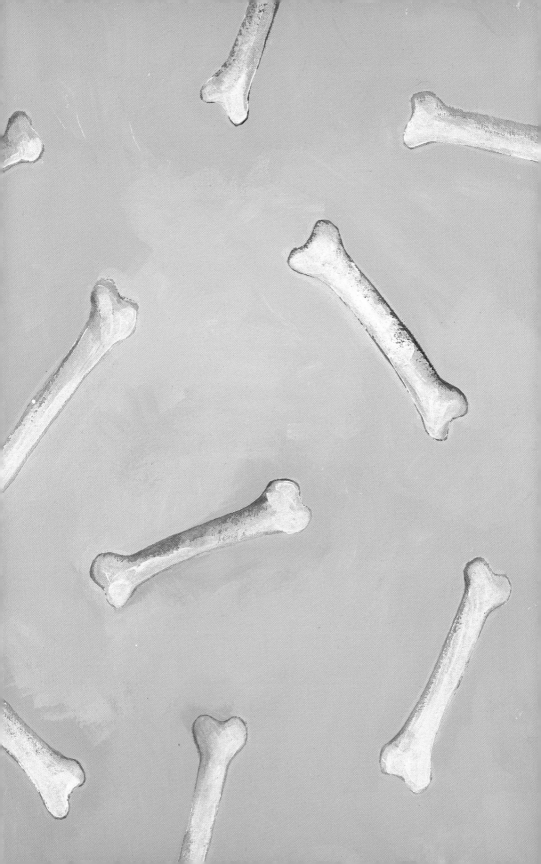

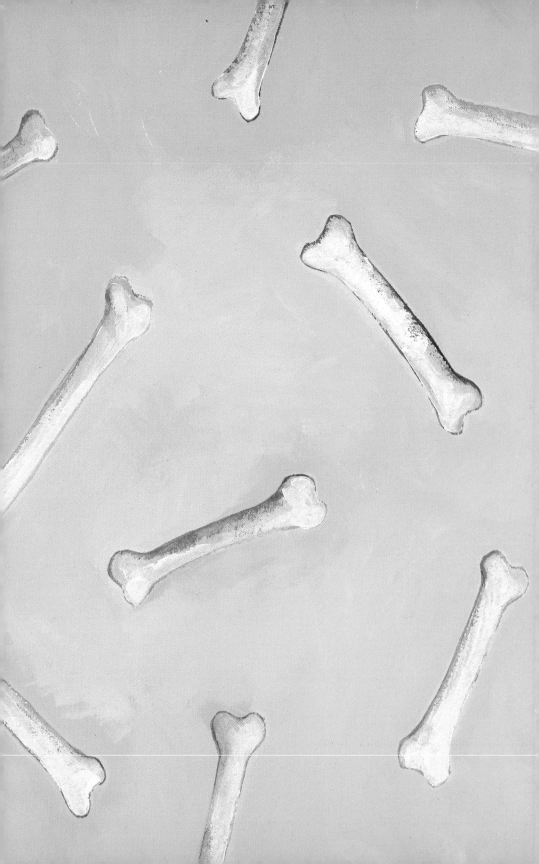